I want a Cat

Ben Hubbard and
Jason Chapman

W
FRANKLIN WATTS
LONDON • SYDNEY

But I think my family are wrong. My friends have cats and they don't wee inside, scratch people, or eat the other pets. I really wish I could change their minds!

My teacher, Mr Jenkins, is also a great cat-lover. Today he gave us a lesson all about cats. He showed us a picture of his cat, Molly.

Then Mr Jenkins gave us some brilliant facts about cats. I made a note of them in my writing book.

After the lesson, I told Mr Jenkins about my family, and how they don't want a cat. Then, he had a brilliant idea. He said I should make a scrapbook about cats and how to look after them. Then my family might let me have one as a pet.

I put Mr Jenkins' cat facts on the first page of my scrapbook!

Cats have a great sense of smell which helps them to make sense of the world around them.

Cats use their whiskers to help feel what is around them, especially when it's dark.

Cats use their tails for balance.

Cats have 30 teeth and a tongue covered with tiny spines to help them take care of their coat.

in

out

Cats can retract their claws when not in use to stop them getting caught on things.

This evening we are visiting our uncle and his cat called Mittens. My brother Alfie and I are going to look after Mittens while my uncle goes away for the weekend. Dad will drive us over each day so we can feed Mittens and keep her company.

I've created different areas for Mittens to climb, explore and hide.

Alfie and I spend some time with Mittens so we get to know each other. My uncle lives on his own so he gives Mittens lots of games and attention. This way she doesn't get bored when he goes out.

Mittens has a scratching post. She can climb up it and sharpen her claws on its thick ropes.

My uncle says this box is Mitten's favourite place. She spends hours jumping in and out and sleeping there. It's just a cardboard box with some holes cut in it but she loves it!

During the weekend, Alfie and I spend time playing with Mittens. It's fantastic fun! My uncle has left us lots of cat toys and we make up some games of our own. We also learn to tell when Mittens doesn't want to play any more as she walks away when she's had enough.

Mittens' favourite game is floor ping-pong. Alfie and I bounce the ping-pong ball to each other and Mittens tries to stop it!

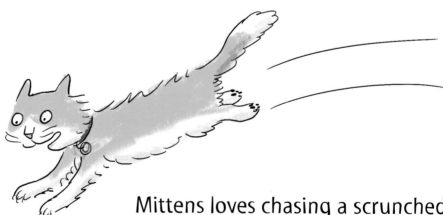

Mittens loves chasing a scrunched-up newspaper ball that Alfie tied to a piece of wool. She pounces on the ball like a tiger in the wild!

We hide a few treats for Mittens around the room and encourage her to find them.

Mittens looks as if she's tired and has had enough for now. Let's stop playing for a while.

My uncle's tips for cat play:

Don't let a cat play with your fingers or toes or it will teach her bad habits. Instead let her chase, bite and scratch her toys.

All cats need to scratch and it's important to give them a scratching post so they don't do it on the sofa!
You can buy or make your own post, or provide pieces of carpet to scratch.

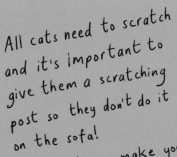

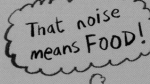

 MITTENS

That noise means FOOD!

Cats can be trained to come to your call by rewarding them when they arrive.

Mr Jenkins is taking us on a class trip to a cat rehoming centre. There are loads of different cats there: males, females, kittens, adults, pedigree cats and Moggies. Pedigrees are cats with parents of the same breed. Moggies come from a real mixture of cats. At the rehoming centre, a cat expert called Jenny gives a talk.

Kittens can purr soon after they've been born. They purr and 'paddle' on their mum to help get her milk. Cats purr when they are happy and content, but can also purr when they are scared, in pain or ill.

Cats like to save energy by resting and sleeping for about 16 hours a day. This is why they like their cat naps.

Cats in the wild like to hunt at dawn and dusk so your cat may be awake early in the morning while you're still asleep.

Jenny's advice for cat care:

All cats need to be fed and cared for. They need to be taken to the vet when they are sick and for regular health checks and vaccinations.

Kittens need a lot of care when they are growing up and somebody needs to be around to look after them.

Adult cats need to have someone around each day, at least in the morning and evening.

Jenny from the rehoming centre gave me some information about cat body language for my scrapbook. Cats 'speak' using their bodies, making sounds and scents. Alfie helps me print off some cat body language pictures from the Internet.

Scared

A scared cat crouches on the ground, flattens her ears, opens her eyes wide and tucks her tail around her body.

It's best to leave a scared cat alone and not try to touch her or stare at her.

Relaxed

A relaxed cat will look you in the eye to show that she trusts you and feels safe. She may also sprawl out on the floor to show she is happy for you to stroke her.

Today is International Cat Day. Cat owners everywhere are posting photos and videos of their cats online and explaining why they love them.

Always choose a cat with the right character traits for you. Check your home, lifestyle and family suits this cat's needs.

A vet from a Cat Friendly Clinic posts a photo with his Moggy, Shadow. He says Shadow has a great personality. A cat's personality is made up of how she behaves, thinks and feels.

The whole family loves looking at the online cats. Even Dad and Grandad smile a lot and point at the ones they like the best.

Suki is a pedigree cat who loves shoes.

Aggie is also a pedigree cat. She has a big personality and always wants to be in charge!

Jodie is a friendly moggy who loves being tickled.

There's some great personalities coming across on International Cat Day. Some are pedigree cats. These are a particular breed so tend to look alike and have similar character traits. All cats need health care but sometimes a pedigree cat may need a bit extra such as more grooming if they have a long coat.

After International Cat Day, I decide to look at some cat types on the Internet and print off some pictures. All cats have different personalities but the breeds have some character traits in common.

BENGAL

BRITISH SHORTHAIR

An energetic hunter that looks like a leopard and needs a large garden to roam in.

An easy-going cat that often likes attention and doesn't need much grooming.

BURMESE

MAINE COON

A big-eyed cat that makes lots of vocal sounds and usually loves people.

A gentle giant who has a long coat and loves hunting in the garden.

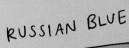

TURKISH VAN

RUSSIAN BLUE

A strong cat with a silky coat and furry paws. He or she needs lots of grooming.

A grey cat with green eyes that likes routine and can sometimes be shy.

Moggies are the most common pet cat. They come in all sorts of shapes, colours and sizes and have different character traits and personalities. They can also suffer from fewer health problems than pedigree cats. I think I like Moggies the best!

THREE OF MY FAVOURITE MOGGIES

MEOW

My auntie and cousin Jack have taken in a pregnant foster cat. She has given birth to a litter of kittens. Jack has been introducing them to new people. This is called 'socialisation'.

Today, Mum and I are spending the day with them. Jack wants the kittens to meet four new people every week to help them to be comfortable around different people.

They know how to use the litter tray already!

Jack says cats are clean creatures which are careful about going to the toilet. Many kittens learn to use their litter tray by watching their mum but Jack is helping by gently putting the kittens in the tray after they eat, sleep and play.

Jack says the kittens are now eating four small meals of kitten food a day. This means someone always has to be around to feed them. They also need fresh water daily.

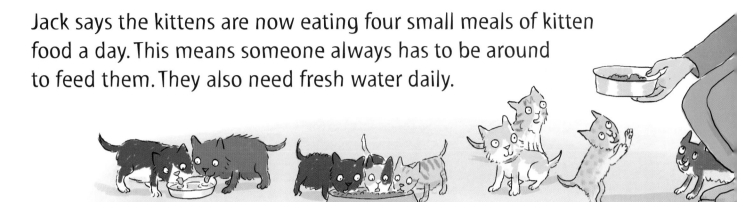

Jack gave me a great advice leaflet for looking after cats. I put it in my scrapbook.

CAT DOS AND DON'TS

ALWAYS be quiet and gentle with a cat.

LEAVE your cat alone while she is sleeping or eating.

ALWAYS let a cat come over to you in her own time and let her move away from you if she wants to.

Today, Mum and I are helping to take Jack's kittens to be neutered, vaccinated and microchipped so they're ready to find new homes. Their mum is going to be neutered too so she doesn't become pregnant again. We fill the kittens' cat carriers with their blankets so it will be cosy and smell like them. We cover the carriers with another blanket so they can't see out.

Going to the vet can be stressful for cats and kittens but you were well prepared!

The vet says all kittens need vaccinations at nine and twelve weeks of age and boosters in the future. These protect against cat diseases, and a kitten shouldn't be let outside until she has had all of them.

The vet shows us how to groom a cat. Cats should be groomed from a young age. Cats with long hair need extra grooming!

Vet

Caring for your new Cat

MICROCHIPPING

All cats should be microchipped. This is when a small microchip is injected into the scruff of a cat's neck. The microchip has all of a cat's information in case she gets lost.

NEUTERING

Cats should be neutered. This is an operation that should take place no later than four months of age and stops cats having kittens. It is important for the well-being of your cat and can also help to stop unwanted behaviour such as unneutered male cats wandering off in search of female cats.

HEALTH CHECKS

Ensure your cat has annual health checks and is regularly treated for fleas and worms throughout the year.

Mum seems to be coming round to the idea of having a pet cat. But Dad is still not sure. He wonders if our house will be safe for a cat. Luckily, I have some information from the vet on making a home 'cat proof'.

In our kitchen, Dad and I see loads of things like plastic bags and cleaning products that could harm a cat. These would need to be put away in a secure cupboard. We would also have to 'cat proof' the other rooms in our house, as well as the shed and garage.

A new cat would need her own space with a 'hidey hole' to make her feel safe while she adjusts to our home. The spare room would be perfect. It's quiet with space for food and water bowls, a litter tray and a scratching post.

A cat needs:

A **cat bed with a blanket**. Pet shops sell cat beds but you can make one from a cardboard box with one side cut off.

A **litter tray** for a cat to go to the toilet in. These need to be regularly cleaned and kept somewhere quiet so that your cat has privacy while she uses it.

A **cat carrier** to bring your cat home in and take her to the vet's. A plastic and wire carrier with a lid on top is best.

A tall and stable **scratching post** to help keep her claws in good condition.

Today we're in for a treat. The whole family is visiting the cats at the rehoming centre. Jenny shows us around.

Mum, Dad and Alfie spend all of their time with the kittens, but there is an older cat who wants to be my friend. After only a few minutes, it feels like we've known each other for years!

I always thought I'd like a kitten for a pet, but now I'm not so sure. Jenny said kittens are a lot of work and need more time and effort than adult cats.

Then, there was as even better surprise waiting for me in the spare room. It's the cat from the rehoming centre!

I hope my scrapbook has provided lots of information about having a cat as a pet. Here's some advice which I found the most helpful:

Cats need to have things that allow them to be a cat. Then they can do the things that cats like to do, such as jumping, climbing, scratching, chasing pouncing and snoozing.

Don't let a cat play with your fingers or toes as this will teach her bad habits. Instead use wand or fishing-rod type toys to keep hands out of the way and also let her chase, pounce and grab her own toys.

Getting a cat from a rehoming centre is a terrific way of giving a cat in need a new home.

Cats show us when they are scared, relaxed or frustated through their body language. Watching a cat's body language can help you better understand her.

All cats have different personalities and it's important to choose a cat who is a good match to your family. It's also important to choose a cat who will be happy living with you.

There are lots of different breeds of pedigree cat, but many people simply choose a Moggy for a pet.

Kittens need somebody around constantly to care for them when they are young.

All cats need to be neutered, vaccinated and microchipped as well as having regular health checks at the vet and treatments for fleas and worms.

All cats need a cat-proof home with a bed in a quiet space that they can call their own.

All cats need a hidey hole where they can go away and hide when they're worried to help them feel safe and secure.

An adult cat makes just as good a pet as a kitten.

BATTERSEA DOGS & CATS HOME

Battersea Dogs & Cats Home is a famous rescue centre which looks after over 3,000 cats and 7,000 dogs every year. Battersea has centres in London, Berkshire and Kent that never turn away a cat or a dog in need. Over 1,000 volunteers, carers and nurses look after the animals and help find them new homes.

CAT IDENTIFICATION

A cat should wear a quick release collar (which snaps open if she gets caught in something) with an engraved ID tag with her owner's name and address on it. A cat should also be microchipped and remember to keep your address details updated when you move.

INSURANCE

Pet insurance is recommended to cover the cost of vet bills.

Visit the Battersea website at: battersea.org.uk

GLOSSARY

CAT-PROOF
Ready and safe for a cat.

FOSTER CAT
When a cat is taken care of by a family for a short period of time. This prepares them for their permanent home by getting them used to a new lifestyle and to being handled by people.

HOUSETRAINED
Trained to go to the toilet in a litter tray.

LITTER
A number of young animals born at the same time to one female cat. There are usually between three and five kittens in a litter. (Also litter tray – see housetrained.)

MOGGY
Also known as a non-pedigree cat, a Moggy is a cat that is not a pedigree or is not from a recognised breed.

MICROCHIPPED
Inserting a small microchip with an owner's detail into the scruff of a cat's neck.

NEUTERING
An operation which stops a cat from having kittens.

PEDIGREE
A cat which has been born from parents of the same breed.

REHOMING CENTRE
A place that takes stray or unwanted pets and finds them new homes.

VACCINATION
A treatment to protect against disease.

Franklin Watts
First published in Great Britain in 2017
by The Watts Publishing Group

Illustrations copyright © Jason Chapman, 2017
Text copyright © Franklin Watts, 2017

All rights reserved.

Produced under licence from Battersea Dogs Home Ltd.
Battersea Dogs & Cats Home

Royalties from the sale of this book go towards supporting the
work of Battersea Dog & Cats Home (Registered charity no 206394)
battersea.org.uk

Credits
Editor: Sarah Peutrill
Design: Sophie Pelham
Cover design: Peter Scoulding

The Author and Publisher would like to thank the staff of
Battersea Dogs & Cats Home for their guidance with this book.

HB ISBN: 978 1445 1 5068 0
PB ISBN: 978 1445 1 5070 3

Printed in China

Franklin Watts
An imprint of
Hachette Children's Group
Part of The Watts Publishing Group
Carmelite House
50 Victoria Embankment
London EC4Y 0DZ

An Hachette UK Company
www.hachette.co.uk
www.franklinwatts.co.uk

Molly

I ♥ CATS

by Holly

Picture credits: Africa Studio/Shutterstock: 11br, 29b, 32bl. Tony Campbell/Shutterstock:
17bc. chombosan/Shutterstock: 21bl. Ysbrand Cosijn/Shutterstock: 5b, 29tl. Hanna Darzy/
Shutterstock: 17tr. g215/Shutterstock: 16br. Iola 1960/Shutterstock: 11bc, 29tr. Eric Isselee/
Shutterstock: 17br. Jojosmb/Shutterstock: 16bl. JRP Studio/Shutterstock: 19b. I Kasparus/
Shutterstock: 16tr. Light Hound Pictures/Shutterstock: 15tr. Rob McKay/Shutterstock: 15tl.
Katho Menden/Shutterstock: 17bl. Olesya Nakipova/Shutterstock: 16tl. Okssi/Shutterstock:
23bc. Vadim Petrakov/Shutterstock: 17tl. Sashatigar/Shutterstock: 21br. Shutterstock: 21bc.
JJ Sniper/Shutterstock: 11bl, 29c. Jakub Zak/Shutterstock: 15c, 28bl. Every attempt has been
made to clear copyright. Should there be any inadvertent omission please apply to the
publisher for rectification.